ZOUNDS!

Poems

Aleksander Zywicki

Barrow Street Press
New York City

Cover Photo: Kellice Swaggerty
Cover Design: Catherine Charbonneau
Interior Design: Michelle Caraccia

Published 2025 by Barrow Street, Inc., New York City
(501) (c) (3) corporation. All contributions are tax deductible.
Distributed by:
Barrow Street Books
c/o University of Rhode Island
English Department, Swan 114
60 Upper College Road
Kingston, RI 02881

Barrow Street Books are distributed by Itasca Books Distribution & Fulfillment, 210 Edge Place, Minneapolis MN, 55418, itascabooks.com. Telephone (844) 488-4477; amazon.com; Ingram Periodicals Inc., 1240 Heil Quaker Blvd, PO Box 7000, La Vergne, TN 37086-700 (615) 213-3574; and Armadillo & Co., 7310 S. La Cienega Blvd, Inglewood, CA 90302, (310) 693-6061.

Special thanks to the University of Rhode Island English Department and especially the PhD Program in English, 60 Upper College Road, Swan 114, Kingston, RI 02881, (401) 874-5931, which provides valuable in-kind support, including graduate and undergraduate interns.

First Edition

Library of Congress Control Number: 2025944960
ISBN: 978-1-962131-11-7

for my families

CONTENTS

I.

II.

III.

IV.

I've known a Heaven, like a Tent—
To wrap its shining Yards—
Pluck up its stakes, and disappear—
Without the sound of Boards
Or Rip of Nail— Or Carpenter—
But just the miles of Stare

—Emily Dickinson

Poet, I beg of you,
By the God you never knew, help me out of this Denmark
Which threatens to go from bad to worse

—"Canto I" of *The Inferno,* Dante Alighieri
Translated by Mary Jo Bang

I.

the sign of the cross

in the name of the forehead
& of the sternum & of the left
& right shoulders respectively

& sometimes improvised
with lips at the end & a pinch
of nothing held to the sky

& sometimes mirrored
the shape drawn in plumes
of smoke & ceremony

& sometimes twitched
over & again a compulsion
to ward off tragedy

dialing God they called it
when they taught me
crossing yourself as though

way up upon a tightrope
strung between
the common tongue

& prayer we walk
to bless the body
as with a spell

an alchemy not
otherwise afforded
to such ordinary hands

whatever it is called
it is always Easter
in the picture where

my dead father has risen
his arm to hang
the wrenching Christ

above our dinner table
& my eyes like wounds
are always opened

as if with dreadful secrecy
I had witnessed blood
dripping into the food

home cooking

I was raised on milk my brother
on water though he'd have you believe
that he was brought up on blood & I
on butter—but it was childhood
my dear with all its glow & horror & no
amount of honey or thunder will change
the careful attention your sons pay
to the way you feed your daughters

childhood is the kingdom where nobody dies

for Cory Leadbeater

when a child is visited
a long time by death
& death decides to leave

he feels abandoned
& inclined to stare off
at gnats scattered above

the hillside wishing
he could join them
& bite the flesh off

of the skulls he finds
in the grass this is what
he knows long before

any one of his friends
though they soon will know
too but in their own way

& not his & when
they do find out
they will ask him how

he could withhold this
which could have been
known to them sooner

& he will stick out his tongue
to reveal a swarm making
black what was pink

misgive & mistake

suddenly it is the hour
when God is peeled from your tongue
when your beloved is similarly peeled
because their love is nothing
a saltless eye
a calloused hand

you switch off the light
it is possible you don't know
how to want anything

some die from this
some grow old
& die from this

the vision

my father knew
he was dying knew
the pocky ulcers

that coiled & climbed
his legs would fang
their venom through

the night & that he'd be
devoured shadow bone
& all by morning

he said so again
& again as though
no one could hear

him behind
the door my mother
closed on them

*

I was not afraid though
only ten I could by
that time chart

his agonized bark
as faithfully as any EKG
could sketch a mountain

range stretched within
me so often did
our house rise

& collapse with quaking
of his lungs
that the silence I knew

to lend his howl
relief could be
conjured by heart

*

at dawn in the exhaust
of the ambulance
I still could not believe

even as I watched
as he was lifted & packed
by able men & rolled away

I went to the empty space
his body left & schemed
how I might not now

have to be the one
to revolve the iron spokes
of his chair to go on

pushing him any further
through what I could see
for the first as being my life

*

& how my septic
brain swelled
in pools of greed

as my thoughts
turned to the morning
announcement biting

through the tender ears
of my fourth-grade class
that I had been made

new & special
by grief & how
they would then be told

to bow their heads
clasp their hands
& pray for me

*

when it happened finally
& my face was taken
& pressed into

the heaving chest
of my brother
I saw in that dark

the shape I'd continue
to see all my life
a vision of my self

identical in almost
every way save for
how he could sob

with full-throated ease
because he never wanted
his father to die

bullseye

as I imagine
the tree in Eden
is dead in the heart

dead in the heart
is a way of saying
in the center

in the eye too
there are times
when I take you

in through the eye
& feel dead
in the heart

of my life
& there are times
when I don't

& then it is not
only you but I
who am missing

marriage

in the rooms we rent
the floors are old

the bowed slats swell
with heat & shrink

with cold at odd
hours releasing

unseen snares for
our uneven feet

we fetch the needle
clean it with a candle

go digging through
the other's skin

returning at times
with the expected

at others
a bloody fragment

neither
could predict

as the omen goes

it is true even if it doesn't seem so
the bird came in the window
& couldn't let go of itself
as a thing that shouldn't be in a room

the empty room not empty
the classroom emptied of students
a room with dirty windows
that grant the sky a tree on occasion

the bird is of these & knows it
batters its body against what it sees
as itself as the way out but isn't
is just more room more window

the years that followed
were the worst of my life
the mornings browned by evening
& hanged over my fire escape garden

telling me to leap
through the glass of the window
the clean window I'd crush
against in the attempt

I am of these I know it
there were nights I would walk
through shoals of cherry blossoms
hand in hand with my delusion

that this is not my life
in the shoals too were your feet
no trick of glass no mirror yours
you were part of this delusion

I'd crush against
in the worst years
the years that followed the bird
the omen the walls the windows

discipline

hope is the regenerating
liver of Prometheus picked
clean by the scavenging
beak & always at 3 a.m. when

the gorge is most still
& the sound of gnashing
travels to the thresholds
of unseen sleepers

alive now to the dark
arena of small horrors
where they lie warm
cocooned by ruin

kissing the boy in church

I can hardly even picture it now—
the face of God I expected to see

on the statue of the baby the other
children & I had lined up in church

to kiss between each peck two nuns
took turns wiping the mouth of Christ

with Lysol gently & absentmindedly
stripping paint from his lips until lips

miraculously vanished as the body does
did I imagine that—had they remained

—they would've parted to smile or speak
or only that they would be there & that

I too would have the chance to decorate
his mouth with my own

stickerbook

in the stickerbook
made to look like a house
where the stickers are all
the things that go in a house

there are grayed-out spaces
my daughter calls shadows
in the shape & in the places
where the stickers are to go

there is a grayed-out shape
of a teapot on the stove
that is not grayed out &
the grayed-out shape of a woman

sitting across a table that is not
grayed out from an old man
who is not grayed out
& not drinking tea either

because she is not there
to make it for him to fill
the kettle shadow space
on the stove or she is

making it but not for him
in the grayed-out house
of shadows in the shapes of all
the things that go in a house

the house on Zabriskie

after he died the crack
in the ceiling deepened
in color & grew longer

then the flood came
& we waded & bailed
waded & bailed &

shouted omens
& economics at each
other while mail

gathered on the dining
room table spilling
his name onto the floor

we passed a year
this way slamming
the screen door to cast

each other more starkly
in our torment
& on the way out

catching sight
of the bulbs he planted
reaching in the shape

of fingers breaking
through the ground
as if begging for rain

time hex
after Paul Celan

autumn again eating
out of my palm

misses the treat
& eats the hand

gets a taste for me
it doesn't despise

& eats some more
I may be dead or

I may die watching
eternity dissolve

in time it is Thursday
& I am full of holes

a wind could blow
through a wind

to blast about what is
spent as brown leaves

& never rests
suspended in

decline & pierced
by flex of sun

falling toward
the paw I open

to the greedy wind
the gaudy trees

II.

making the shape

for John Brennan, longshoreman

that my great grandfather
ate roach poison in June
of '49 & that his son

a newlywed a veteran
of the Battle of the Bulge
drove him to the hospital

& watched him die
has been known all
the while what is still

uncertain & is only now
being considered in light
of the research conducted

for the making of this poem
is that he may not have
intended his suicide

*

that the daily rite
of submitting himself
in the open air

to the geometry
of huddled bodies
waiting to trade

their yet unearned
wages for the mere
chance at labor

instead of drowning
in drink or jumping
into the Hudson

was called by their
debtors & hirers
making the shape

*

that the longshoremen
belonging to this
devotional crisis

pitting dignity against
hunger reason
against the mob

did hook their tongues
into this bastard
idiom hauling it up

onto the docks cleaned
of scorn—every man
in the shape knew

that this phrase more
truly meant to ascend
to become

*

that through my mother
make the shape are
the only words I had

ever known for certain
he had said until
the slender rectangle

printed in *The Jersey*
Journal: "Man Dies
of Poison" boasting

a statement he made
to a reporter one hour
before his death: he "took

the poison by mistake"
—what else
could he really say

*

that my mother has
taken this to mean
that her grandfather

did not prove
a *desperate soul*
is one way

of making the shape—
that the article offering
this condolence could

not pry such craft
from his driver's mouth
but ends with "the son

could not be found"
is what could also be
meant by this phrase

our lady of the blasted stump

lightning did not shape her
but someone else in town
saw as you did & put flowers
by what are not her feet

& now the illusion is carved
deeper into the hearts
of others as more grocery
store flowers arrive each day

& not just flowers rosaries
that dangle miraculously
from invisible fingers
prayers folded & stuffed

into the trunk sometimes
a bottle of golden brown
piss an offering even you
can't help but think profane

it's just a hole you want
to shout just someone
cutting the rot out to keep
the feeble thing living

but every time you do
your forked tongue
is stilled by weight
of feet that are not feet

& the flowers as if
plucked from a plastic
Eden applaud with
rustling of their bags

heathen driven to his knees

the first images of Earth seen
from space were humiliating

all our blue in all that black
a perfect bruise pointless

in every way brazen science
seemed then to be saying

now like the many-lidded eyes
of frogs their shutters snap

nebulas & galactic clusters auld
& weird as the crystalline sphere

of Dante & the red human heart
thumps not more than a beat

too long about it the same red heart
that dangles in the pencil-thin

outline of the human body seen
in pharmaceutical commercials

where planet-like in its oneness
it is shown to feel pain

in a flash of angry red lines
& all around it is empty space

empty to sell the heart its medicine
sure but empty also as space

was thought to be empty
in science's old hat images

& not just empty hostilely so
indifferent even

through great shows of felt pain
& ecstatic flashes of the heart

tonight as the tails of comets
& detonations of every kind

sail senselessly through the pitch
I reach for what I mean

to be prayer but is not
is the empty space around

emptied not of language
but of its healthful medicine

where godlessly I thump
my red one in pain for yours

vows

I keep hoping for better habits
to love within my means
to sow in spite of havoc
to want less of what I need

to sow in spite of havoc
to forgive myself the cost
to want less of what I need
to grow from shapeless loss

to forgive myself the cost
to relish in having spent
to grow from shapeless loss
to go where going went

to relish in having spent
what I knew when I had it
to go where going went
& give thanks as it happens

what I'll know when I have it
what I'd sown in spite of havoc
I'll give over to what must happen
& keep hoping for better habits

the birthday party

the man was 40
& we had eaten

& we were splitting up
some of us to see

the pink moon & some
on a liquor run & right

there dead in the heart
of 5th Avenue you put

your lips in your hand
& pressed them with

a flower's strength
a kiss you meant for me

& sent it stumbling
to my foolish cheeks

puffed & blooming
with sudden roses

made from your shade
a kind of moon pink

hope is a discipline

I know what I am
& yet sometimes I catch
myself walking from room

to room with fists
full of dead flowers
trying in vain

to keep the blooms
going so far as to plunge
them over & again

into cups of new water
expecting more
than indifference

to issue
from my touch
but I lord

my suffering
over my love
of others

whose love
is only as good
as it makes me feel

crossing myself

my mother sent me a Father's Day card
five months before my daughter

is due & I won't even get the baby baptized
for her I think she is afraid the love

my wife & I have won't be enough—
& how could it be compared

to what we won't be giving her
Longinus is the name given to the soldier

who pierced the side of Jesus to make
sure he was dead I was picked to play

him once in a school pageant & I suspect
that that's part of her concern too

that some men are called to carry the cross
& some to stab the already crucified

& that without a God-sized love
my daughter won't be able to see

every stranger hanging there fixed
at the ordinates of the past

they shoulder into the latitude
of every present moment & have

decency enough not to stick
her blade into their side

maybe she won't or maybe
she'll search herself for a name

for the dead man she doesn't know
on the first crucifix she finds

marveling at the state of his corpse
so ordinary in death but alive

coming to me

I run things into the ground
I know it & I know you
do too having been put
there as in a shallow

grave while I disappeared
to ride the wheels off
of something else
in your stead every

enemy I have I know
damn well I have
made for myself
by sparing the rod

& spoiling rotten
I deserve nothing
not a God not a gray
sky to put it in

finches maybe

in the woods where I walk
there are birds

I don't know what kind of birds
I don't know what they eat

I see them in the same place
along what has become a routine

path for me lifting with their beaks
what seems a heroic bulk

of leaves (first to the left of them
then to the right) as though

looking for something small
a key I see them do it again

& again (first to the left then right)
during what has become a routine

first rain

for Eva Fay, six days old

November now & after
this there'll be less
to look at in the trees

what is gentle for me
& I hope for you in
your thin sleep is out

there presently throwing
to Earth the gold dead
things that just days ago

seemed to relish announcing
your birth & now cede
as ancestors their gifts

to the wet sod
you cannot know their joy
as the gnarled witch fingers

of remaining branches pass
over your still storm-gray
eyes but as you step

unevenly in the spring
their sweet decay will make
the wind smell good

holy ghost

sent home from seminary
with a body even God
could not help but curse

my father lived
as so many do
orbiting the shape

of his life
like a man caught
in the cold ballet

of space haplessly
twirling as dazzling
vessels vanished

all around him
& dead stars burned
for someone else

*

the earth
into which he dug
the tip of his cane

was to him
as his own corpse
—an insult

at his expense—
for though it flowered
endlessly the stems

seemed always
to extend laughing
from wells

that were his
eyes & to sway long
in the terrible wind

*

one by one like
knockoff gems
he prevailed in amassing

the sacraments—
placed a diamond
ring on my mother's

finger & bowed
his head as the bishop
ordained him—

all while listening
as though in some
deep pocket

the chintzy trinkets
failed to form what
wouldn't save him

*

& together much
unhappily they contrived
to put his body

everywhere he feared
he mightn't ever enjoy
the privilege of being

so that he could sit
certain he had
conquered

each remote locale
& atop every unpuzzled
stair recite

to the sky
the same handful
of angry prayers

*

an adoration for
for soil staining
his children's hands

a blessing for
surrogate joy
ringing in other men

repentance for
always his
mutant pride

thanksgiving
that each body
is free to die

& like all poor Christian
souls supplication only
ever for more & more

III.

joy in the valley

little gold watch
all you want
is my time

little gold watch
all you want
is my eyes

& for you
to be in them
as they bleat

joy as in a valley
that echoes joy
& believes it is

happy last night
you would not sleep
stuck your pacifier

in my mouth
& looked happy
it was all

that was yours
to give & you gave
it to me with force

little gold watch
that won't let me
check the time

his like again

chaos gathers each night
into the ghost of my father
he's furious at my family

& believes I can prove that
I love him by getting even
which I've come to realize
could mean almost anything

so I rattle my tail
& make sure to be seen
sharpening my fangs half

hoping to one day coil
into oblivion half hoping
to one day be trampled
by a callus on a holy heel

the joke in *Hamlet*

about Fortune being a prostitute
is that for Rosencrantz & Guildenstern

to get lucky they'd have to pay for it
I thought I understood having been

knocked out on the playground
by the boyfriend of the first girl

I'd kissed but I know now
that Fortune must get tired

having for centuries to put the light back
in the hollow of every eye She meets

that She just doesn't want to hang
around too long after each encounter

to coo sweet sounds to idiots
& promise Her love for a lifetime

how do you get to Carnegie Hall

on days I don't hear
from you I practice
that you're dead

& it goes just how
I know it will all day
long   not a word

& I tell myself
over & over like
someone in hell

it is because you're dead
you're dead I yell
to myself you're dead

because I know if
I don't start now
I'll never be ready

devotion

some wells
some ordinary wells

exist for you to drag
the moon up in

a bucket even
though you forget

to do it every night
& so the moon

doesn't rise & some
wells all they do

is punish you
with the scraping

sound your moonless
cup makes upon

their floors a practice
you somehow

keep faithfully & keep
the neighbors up well

I've had it cover all
the wells who could

stand a baby falling
into one cover

your own throat even
if you are to remain

parched in unblinking
dark again anyway

how it goes

I say how'd you sleep did you dream
& she says yeah & I say what did
you dream about & she says animals

& I say animals what were they
doing & she says sleeping & I say
on the next day how'd you sleep did

you dream & she says baby ducks
& I say baby ducks what were they
doing & she says swimming & moves

her finger to mime swimming
but looks instead like she's casting
a spell & the next day I ask

if she's dreamed & she says yeah
& I ask about what & she says dada
& I say yeah thinking she's asking

me a question & she says no dada
& I realize that's she's saying it's me
she's dreamed & I ask

what was I doing & she says walking
& I do not disturb what becomes silence
between us with further question

for as sure as animals sleep & ducks
swim in this place where I had not
walked before I am now walking

& I do not know if I have the heart
to learn if I have been cast in her
midnight spell as someone

who walks to or from her
& for how long & to what end
& then I say yeah & she says yeah

long after

in these woods
are shadows
tracks & me

disappointed
which I seem always
to be at least always

when I am with you
& the Earth
all of a sudden

is magnificent
& large like these trees
old & full of importance

& magnificent to walk
through as though
meant for someone

else better I think
in those moments to be
a shadow something

already gone having
left behind only
tracks that point

to where I might be
hiding or sleeping or
waiting for you

you
for whom the Earth
must always be this way

if you love me let me have it

the gold balloons inflated
        into the digits of the new
year now twelve days old
        & tied to some part of the self-
checkout kiosks at CVS
        are sinking hard not to
see them as weighted by
        all that gold—the promise
of it the richness easy
        to see their inevitable decline
as emblematic of gaunt days
        ahead a reluctant part
of me feels encouraged
        by their glacial droop
to be fine in my own ugliness
        to welcome shadows crossing
over my face to have nerve
        & spine enough to hang
on to what lasts of my hate
        hard not to think of hate
as the perfect place of the heart
        easy to imagine it as a failed
attempt at indifference—
        as gravity on something gold

we don't talk 10 years now

sometimes he would see that I don't
like being with him & he would ask me
if I'm okay & I'd nod & say just tired
but he wouldn't let it go he'd push

he'd say why are you so tired all the time
& I'd give reasons for tiredness
that do not hint at simply how
I do not like being with him

& he'd find ways to pin all
the reasons for tiredness that I had
given him in place of the truth

to some flaw in me or another as his
brain would storm up more & more
ways out of the tiredness I was in

*

& one morning after a good night
he called me to ask what I was doing
with my life & didn't I see how I was

spoiling that I had spoiled that I was
rot was rotten & that that was what
would allow me to have good times

even as I cast the magnificent promise
of the moment I didn't deserve anyway
into the furnace of right now it's that

I was rotten & didn't I see how ripe
a thing must be to rot how hospitable
to maggots how welcoming of a hot sun

that shouldn't have bothered shining on
a thing that'd just waste it as it wastes all

*

& sometimes I'd fawn bring gifts
feign excitement in his presence
bruise my knees on the marble floors
of chapels to show him I could

change that I'd prayed we could
be more loving to each other
that the harm was not my own
but of my own making

& carried with it a maker's mark
in the shape of a shame
I would now willingly wear

to show myself for the monster
I am to a world that would after
all these years know the truth

*

& sometimes I'd really try to talk
to him like someone who can be
talked with you know like anyone

can be talked with like anyone
you can find in your phone
dial up at random & talk

to them & say listen here I am
this is my gesture extended
in good will & exhaustion to mend

it the big gash in us I might have
caused & that you might have
caused & I'd leave that last part out

really praying now that reason
& sweetness could be the things

*

but there is no talking with him only
barking not barking like a dog &
not like the barking of its cruel master

but the barking of a man who is also
crawling the way a dog might barking
& foaming about the mouth the way
a dog might under the cruelty of a master

but still not quite
barking cruelly as the master is cruel &
barks but still not quite no it is more

the barking of a man who is crawling like a dog
crawling & foaming about the mouth
because he is in a pain that is his master
a pain that announces itself in barking

*

but I am not a barker & cannot issue
a shriek even one that can compete with all

that & so one day I picked up the phone
& I called to talk as people talk

& instead he barked & foamed in pain
so for a long time I lay next to the phone

& listened to him bark the way a man
in a bed may lie awake all night

while a dog outside of his apartment
somewhere barks with a frenetic energy

that must surely exhaust itself eventually
of all its barking of even its desire

to bark in the first place & yet
it barks & barks & barks & barks

my night alone with the hammer

your enormous face
as though God's
in stone suspended

by thick cables
of twisted metal
dangled before me

you had no eyes
or they were closed
or it didn't matter

your signature
sneer smug like
no one else's

said it was you
said smash me
with a hammer

I looked in my hands
& a hammer I had
without thinking

I set to smashing
cupulas that were
your cheeks

& holes like rubies
into the rich studded
brim of your crown

in the end
the cables held little
left I could call

you & so with
the hammer I struck
my own face again

& again you are
my brother my face
is your face too

IV.

I go to the grave in secret

& only once a year
& usually empty handed
& don't spend much time

& don't say very much
& don't feel half as much
as I ever expect to but last

year nearly crashed my car
punching the passenger
seat turning red yelling

at the point on the bridge
where tires are known to slip
furious with the circles

I'd driven through
the cemetery unable to find
the stone I've visited

for twice as many years
as he's been dead I was
a boy at first & brought

there nowadays fathers
pile up & scatter plot
the yard with earth

tilled atop their old bones
dirt his bones grew old in
how could I not find him

he waits of course for all
things but maybe for me
too & the precious little

I am & offer maybe
he waited for this this
last right when I look

& he is gone for good
& I a man turn red
& crash my car

don't look now

someone is doing with light
what always seems impossible
in paintings throwing beams

but one mainly so that
it seems to call or cradle
the one it touches & no one

else lord let me make it
to the woods before it stops
snowing before they get full

up of people & their dogs
I want to be happy & I am
running out of ideas

& this is one of them
& not something I could
have planned & not

something I could depend
upon why is it always that way
with you but there is a light

or a lightness on those paths
& I want to be in it can't you
hear me I want to be happy

getting to the point

dark this morning
& God is all there is

two wakes this week
& tomorrow a bed

of pain & God
is all there is my son

is grown & does not
know how to live

in his disappointment
in God that is all in God

that simply is he tells me
when he walks down

long city blocks lined
with long city windows

that he does not know
what walks in him

& when I ask if what is
walking is more like all

of this or like just him
he says all of this & I do

not twist this dark knife
dark as all that is

kindling

catechism & Dante
& frescos painted
for cheap by no-name

artists in little churches
scattered across her world
filled the burning lakes

& designed the locking
mechanisms on each
torturer's chamber door

in the vision
of hell my mother
carries around within

her conception
of faith but it is she
who assigns its people

*

& she tells me
the ones she sees
most vividly roiling

in the concentric pit
are not the godless
but the pious

siphons of mercy
in habit & collar
that drank it straight

from the hole
in Christ's hands
& spit out

only timeless bile
& chewed up bits
of brimstone

*

& what I cannot ask
is if the man for whom
she knitted stoles

& strung them around
his neck as he choked
our rooms with smoke

from his censer
on a chain & shaped
our home into a shanty

church full of kneeling
& gospel & blame—
if her deacon husband

isn't also numbered
among the twisting dead
howling in flames

*

& what I ask instead
is if it was not maddening
then to keep faith in a God

as she tended to
this man's momently
collapsing frame

patiently building him
up as if from ash
each morning to serve

as I know she would
wish to serve
if it were not for him

his chair her children
& the house she kept
from catching flame

*

& she says the arms
of God were there
on his most ungrateful

pontific & wrathful
days—arms brimming
with balming grace

even as they gathered
& assembled tinder
out of her dry fortune

arms she knew
would never put her
in the fire & that that

was enough
to be warmed
by their embrace

as downcast angels plead

until your dreams end
know this the hero
who is doomed to perish
in the crumbling tomb

does not know why
he thinks it may be
because of something

he did but he doesn't know
any more than he knows
why he wears t-shirts
and not flowers

but always one to brave
himself for answers
he steps into the mouth

what scripture might well have said

look again at how I make
you shrink & darken & blow
away like an appetite

this arrogance has
its name & its name
is mine this surrender

this slapping of hands
this guessed-at this
fiction this twisted

mouth & sinew go
ahead cry like people
do leave in the day

get into trouble
eat the mountain side
come out on the other

everything beautiful
for its own time
eternity planted

in the human heart
this sulphureous hole
I'm tired of it

this incidental agony
the next time
you want me

bloody just raise
your fist like
everyone else

inconvenient as they are

your granddaughter asks
me are you happy & I say
yeah kiddo I'm happy

& she says why is your face
like this & she mimes
something tortured

a face seen in woodgrain
& I say I'm sorry kiddo
& she says make this

& she smiles like someone
in a book that shows
children how to smile

& so I smile & her smile
widens & shortly after
the night eases & she sleeps

in the Magritte painting
memory is the silver ball
that's cracked the temple

of antiquity & made her
bleed but you & I know
it is no toy this quickening

like tunnels formed
by blood through sand
memory is a dead thing

made to wheeze again
convulsions of longing
toothless crimson joy

the man who died in the cold

on a television on a television cart
a man without imagination
picks up his last matchstick
with his teeth & draws it across
his leg nearly twenty times
before he succeeds in lighting it
singeing the hairs of his nostrils
coughing up sulfur & dropping
the match in the snow
but before he freezes to death

I hit pause & ask the class
about imagination & at first
they say it means to picture
yourself & then they talk
about it as a place you can go
but then a boy raises his hand
to say that it is just a tool
you can use to solve problems
in a tone that sounds like
he's already watched to the end

not a dream moving

I woke & you were looking
over your nude shoulder

at me through time but
who could say how much

as if you were one
in a painting called *bathers*

looking through oil
& dripping riverwater

onto the marble floor
of the museum where I

stood too long ears back
as though on the banks

I had paused unsure
if to answer your look

paschal pandemic

it was also spring
& from the window
of our quarantine
the yard appeared
to bloom with
the aimless insistence
of a petri dish

& every spring
passed was then in our
controlled environment
slowed to an observable
pace & examined
for variables that
distinguished them

I would think how
we were married
in spring & could
smell if I strained
amid the antibacterial
present something
of that day

did I ask you then
to place your head upon
my chest & listen not
for my heart but for
the sound of a cough
rattling like pills inside
my shell-thin coffer

did we pass that
Easter endeavoring
to see the blue
of the sky
as though it were
the dye & we
lay inside the egg

what feels like a ship but is

my daughter has outgrown her crib
& her grandmother is putting her down
for her last sleep within its city gates

where her infancy will live forever
now without her as she sleeps
in each strange new bed her life

will cradle in while my wife
& I are building outside her
room in complete silence

what feels like a ship but is
the enormous bed of her childhood
which I suppose begins tonight

& whose sleep we sense together
in our marrow will be unlike
this last nap in the kingdom

whose tall walls once flew
banners knitted for her arrival
our apartment so small we hand

each other screws in quiet
to let this sleep happen
sleepwalking almost ourselves

as we make this thing
which seems larger than possible
following the steps as though

we have done this before
like one opening the cellar
door with eyes closed

before walking off the top
to the very bottom
we will not sleep tonight

our eyes will be glued
to the baby monitor to watch
her step off for the first time

the side of her bed
& into the sleeping dark
her nightlight doesn't reach

when she wakes unsure
of where she is
of where we are

of where the life she had
for herself where she knew
herself to be safe has gone

it is hard work keeping
up the silence we know
she needs to sleep

one of us drops the wrench
now & then & the other
glares in noiseless fury

but when we check the monitor
to see how we've disturbed
her we find for the last

our pixilated baby sleeping
on the screen grandma sitting
sentry the ancient city secured

wigilia

this is the night
the dead unbury
themselves & sit

at my table
they do not know
that they are dead

& how would I
convince them
after all I have prepared

according to their taste
the steaming peasant
meal set among

their silverware arranged
with maudlin accuracy
their shining plates

pulled from the attic
& livened their faces
hanging from their picture

frames with the blush
of poinsettias yes
it would appear that all

is too orderly at this
familiar hour in this
strange century as we sit

together again comforted
by the porcelain
eyes of the infant

curled on the sawdust
floor nestled among
his happy & lifeless family

go ahead flash your badges

good, the heart is closed now
as a door against the night, the bolt
dragged along the ravine of my safe-
keeping. now can I unbutton,

unzip. now can I peal the bell
of my hour. now can I be more
than a mouth with which to say yes
with. no one is coming. the door

is shut to the world, to you. closed
now even to me, who cannot rest,
who paces, checks the peephole.
closed tightly now against my ear

that will not listen as I say no
one is coming, sleep. closed
for now, which may, it turns
out, be a very long time.

Notes

Title: The word, *zounds* (s'wounds,) is an Early Modern contraction combining "God's" and "wounds." It appears often in Shakespeare's plays and when it does, it is typically exclaimed as a swear-word intended to flirt with blasphemy. Hamlet says it at Ophelia's graveside as he imagines leaping in to join her corpse. Though, in a literal sense, it is meant to evoke the crucifixion wounds of Christ—I like thinking of it, also, as a word used to classify the wounds sustained in lifelong relationship/struggle with faith.

Page 6: The title, "childhood is the kingdom where nobody dies," is taken from Edna St. Vincent Millay's poem by the same name.

Page 17: During the Feast of the Epiphany, it is common for Catholic children—or, at least it was so at Our Lady of Mount Carmel, in Bayonne, NJ—to celebrate the biblical account of the arrival of the Magi by kissing a statue of the infant Jesus.

Page 20: Paul Celan's "Corona."

Page 25: The title, "making the shape," is drawn from a phrase that emerged out of my great grandfather's career as a longshoreman in Jersey City, New Jersey, during the 1940s. Each day, the dockworkers would assemble in a line called "the shape" or "the shape-up" and wait as their hiring boss assigned jobs to a lucky few. To ensure their employment, many of the workers in the shape would pay either their boss or the mob (to lean on their boss) an advance on the pay they would earn for the chance to work at all. Those few workers who did not compromise their wages or their dignity but continued to stand in line and come by their employment honestly, were said to have "made the shape." In the lives of these men, this phrase would go on to mean something essential about their character. A mourner standing in a long line to pay their respects at a good man's funeral might well think of the length of the line as proof that the dead had "made the shape."

Page 34: The title, "hope is a discipline," is a phrase borrowed from Mariame Kaba.

Page 48: The title, "his like again," is nicked from *Hamlet*: "He was a man, take him for all in all, I shall not look upon his like again" (1.2,195).

Page 49: "the joke in *Hamlet*" comes when Rosencrantz & Guildenstern first attempt to betray Hamlet with small talk: "In the secret part of Fortune? O, most true! She is a strumpet. What news?" (2.2, 253-254).

Page 78: René Magritte, *Memory* (1948).

Page 80: Jack London's, "To Build a Fire," adapted to film in 1969 and narrated by Orson Welles.

Page 87: *Wigilia* is the traditional Polish Christmas Eve vigil supper.

Acknowledgments

Thank you to the editors of the following journals in which some of the poems in this book appeared, often in earlier forms:

Armchair Shotgun: "home cooking"

Bear Review: "stickerbook"

Chicago Quarterly Review: "the birthday party"

Concho River Review: "the man who died in the cold"

Gulf Coast: "devotion"

The Inquisitive Eater: "the sign of the cross," "wigilia"

Landlocked: "heathen driven to his knees"

Laurel Review: "don't look now"

Plume: "go ahead flash your badges"

Right Hand Pointing: "marriage"

Seneca Review: "how do you get to Carnegie Hall," "my night alone with the hammer"

*

Thank you to Kevin Prufer for selecting my book and changing my life.

Thank you to Barrow Street Press for your faith and patience and kindness. My gratitude especially to Rachel Rothenberg, Charles Kell, and Peter Covino.

*

Special thanks to my parents, Betty and Bob, for giving me all the good they have and had within them. It became all the good I have within me. I love you.

Special thanks to Kristin and Eva (and Nora and Nico)—the joy of all my days—for filling my life with peace and tenderness. I love you.

*

Eternal gratitude to Cory Leadbeater, the best and most devoted writer, for all of it—for keeping me alive, for keeping my poems alive, for sneaking me out to toss pebbles up at the mansion's windows.

*

To Mark Bibbins for whom no amount of thanks could ever sufficiently express my gratitude—thank you for so much, but especially: your care, your wit, your kindness, your guidance.

To Camille Rankine, both for the generosity of your words and for teaching me devotion and discipline to the line itself.

To Mr. Jack Campion—before you, no one had ever made me think so hard; no one had ever made my own thoughts so enjoyable to me. Your teaching made me want to devote my life to teaching, which I have. Thank you, Sir, for giving me Shakespeare and Milton, the best and most enduring gifts I've ever received.

To Margery Roby, both for her fidelity and friendship to my mother and for her care in helping me to shake the dust.

To Christopher Halleron, a true man for others, who never once stopped showing up for me.

To John Meredith Hill, who first gave me permission to be a poet. Every "&" is a flower for you.

To Stephen Whitaker, who made me believe in the thing itself. My goodness, thank you.

To everyone at the New School Creative Writing Program, but especially to my teachers: Robert Polito, Elaine Equi, and Laurie Sheck for their generosity, grace, guidance, and genius.

To Christopher Citro and Su Cho and to everyone else at the Martha's Vineyard Institute for Creative Writing for the final nudge that helped get this boulder up the mountain.

To Corinne Viglietta and Peggy O'Brien and everyone at the Folger Shakespeare Library for putting me and my family in touch with the sacred work you do and serve.

To all my students from Bayonne High School, Saint Peter's Preparatory School, Xavier High School, and The Hudson School.

*

To Mathiew Weitman, whose poems I believe in so much more than my own, for your friendship and wisdom.

To Emily Zogbi, Coleman Dues, and Whitney Bard, makers of the shape, for keeping the light in the treehouse on.

To Yasin Ertas, for the extra window I can hang anywhere I go.

To Judith Antelman, for our coffees at the end of the world.

*

To Paul Bailey Dennis Ward, for two decades of friendship and the first photograph of myself I've ever enjoyed.

*

Finally, for all their love and so much more, my undying thanks to: Tony Azzarto, Alex Brumel, Siobhan Casey, Caroline Coppel, Zygfryd S. Dabrowski, Jim DeAngelo, Neil Dingow, Matthew Dougherty, Kevin Dugan, Pete, Jess and Sofia Durning, Michael Friedman, Kevin, Andrea, Padraig, Andriana, and Alanna Friel, Jen Galvao, Maryanne Giovinazzo, Len Gougeon, Caitlin Hickey, Carly Hill, Shawna Hogan, Samantha Horn, Una Hughes, Mary Lou Kowalski, Patty Kroog, Bernard Krzan, Aileen Marcantonio, Matt Mercuri, Raven Migliaccio, Aaron Miller, Pat Morris, Matthew Mulroy, Kathy, John, J.P., Bo and Alma Leadbeater, Tom Murphy, Gerard Nolan, Joshua Perry, Ilaria Perogni, Kaitlyn Pezik, Raquel Rodriguez, Dan Romano, Dominic Scibilia, Justin Scioli, Alex Senatore, Elisabeth Sherman, Evan Simko-Bednarski, Mike Spivack, Kay and Mike Sweeney, Matthew Thomas, Graham Twibell, Javier Vasquez, Dan Ward, Dave Ward, Mr. Brendan Ward, Matt Ward, Natalie Williams, Stefanie Woods, Katherine Wright, Stuart Ziarnik.

Photo by Paul Bailey Denis Ward

Aleksander Zywicki was raised in Bayonne, New Jersey. He holds an MFA from The New School and his work appears in: *Plume*, *Gulf Coast*, *Hunger Mountain*, *Seneca Review*, *Shō Poetry Journal* and elsewhere. Aleks has received a poetry fellowship from the Martha's Vineyard Institute for Creative Writing and a teaching fellowship from the Folger Shakespeare Library. He teaches English and creative writing at The Hudson School.

BARROW STREET PRESS - recent titles:

ZOUNDS! Aleksander Zywicki 2025
Unlikely Skylight, Hollis Kurman 2025
Secret Agent Man, Margot Singer 2025
An Anthology of Rain, Phillis Levin 2025
Spare, Michelle Lewis 2025
The Mouth Is Also a Compass, Carrie Bennett 2024
Brutal Companion, Ruben Quesada 2024
Brother Nervosa, Ronald Palmer 2024
The Fire Road, Nicholas Yingling 2024
Close Red Water, Emma Aylor 2023
Fanling in October, Pui Ying Wong 2023
Landscape with Missing River, Joni Wallace 2023
Down Low and Lowdown..., Timothy Liu 2023
the archive is all in present tense, Elizabeth Hoover 2022
Person, Perceived Girl, A.A. Vincent 2022
Frank Dark, Stephen Massimilla 2022
Liar, Jessica Cuello 2021
On the Verge of Something Bright and Good, Derek Pollard 2021
The Little Book of No Consolation, Becka Mara McKay 2021
Shoreditch, Miguel Murphy 2021
Hey Y'all Watch This, Chris Hayes 2020
Uses of My Body, Simone Savannah 2020
Vortex Street, Page Hill Starzinger 2020
Exorcism Lessons in the Heartland, Cara Dees 2019
American Selfie, Curtis Bauer 2019
Hold Sway, Sally Ball 2019
Green Target, Tina Barr 2018
Luminous Debris: New & Selected Legerdemain, Timothy Liu 2018
We Step into the Sea: New and Selected Poems, Claudia Keelan 2018
Adorable Airport, Jacqueline Lyons 2018
Whiskey, X-ray, Yankee, Dara-Lyn Shrager 2018

For a complete list of publications go to: https://barrowstreet.org